THE FLEUR DE LIS

volume one

THE FLEUR DE LIS

volume one

Emily Isaacson

TATE PUBLISHING & *Enterprises*

The Fleur-de-lis: Volume I
Copyright © 2011 by The Emily Isaacson Institute. All rights reserved.

Published by Tate Publishing & Enterprises, LLC
127 E. Trade Center Terrace | Mustang, Oklahoma 73064 USA
1.888.361.9473 | www.tatepublishing.com

Tate Publishing is committed to excellence in the publishing industry. The company reflects the philosophy established by the founders, based on Psalm 68:11,
"The Lord gave the word and great was the company of those who published it."

Book design copyright © 2011 by Tate Publishing, LLC. All rights reserved.
Cover design by Lauran Levy
Interior design by Stephanie Woloszym

Published in the United States of America

ISBN: 978-1-61663-973-0
1. Poetry / Canadian   2. Fiction / Literary
11.06.21

Good duke, go see if thine walls be high,
And if the door is closed, and archer placed
Within his tower, and go the castle round
Thyself for us; seek in thine arsenal
For armour that will fit—at sixty years...

Victor Hugo

To Prince William
and to the First Nations people

"The hand-made ironwork
on the door of the private
Commons' entrance contains
the fleur-de-lis, the thistle and the rose…"

I passed by two stone lions,
into the inner chamber,
the matchless memorial
of the Peace Tower;
at the door
the handmade
ironwork containing
the fleur-de-lis,
the thistle,
the shamrock,
and the rose
was rumoring lengths
of light,
murmuring measures
of music
under the ornate
gothic gold angels—
tracing my prayers, a subtle verse
in embryonic
hurt
juxtaposed
with liturgy and latitude.

When they sang
in innocent plainsong,
a high purity
reached the gilt glass
ceiling
stenciled in symbols
of Canada, France,
England, Scotland,
Ireland, and Wales...

Justice and Liberty,
icons like saints
in anthem, breathing
through the stained glass:
tracing the water
outline
of the sky.

CONTENTS

FOREWORD

The Fleur-de-lis offers a panoramic investigation of landscapes both spiritual and physical, guiding the reader among the thematic elements of the three volumes. Their collective continuity describes a genre evoking deep imagination for the purpose of facilitating communication between not only the author and reader but persons, nations, and people groups. The art of words, nuance, and poetic device stand out in these free verse pieces, with the poetry as a whole scribing an impressive sensory, sensual universe, a visual documentary in words.

The narrative voice of Volume One bespeaks a deep connection to the institutions and attitudes of the "Old World" even as it shows their interruption by experiences—particularly physical sensations—in the "New World": the Canada at that time.

The new nation that Canada is today develops by way of a transmuting from the old practices of holding to the Commonwealth as opposed to the new practice of independence from this vainglory. The traversing from one world to the next is evidenced in this journey in literature from the old nation to a new nation, in a literal historical voyage from the "Old World" to the new. The primary emphasis for this collection of verse is provided by these two interpretive frames: the idea of nation—and in particular, of the contemporary "breakup" of our old ideas of nation—and the reclaiming of Canadian nationhood by both English, French, and First Nations people. In a sense, it carries a redefinition of what it means personally to be a citizen of this nation and what responsibilities and burdens that belonging carries with it.

In Volume One, where these themes are nascent, one can sense they will emerge and that we will engage with them. However, Volume One carries out other thematic tasks. Written as 222 poems in twenty-two sections, "The Laurel Wreath" highlights poems such as "Myrrh (The Apostle John Observes)" and makes use of the different essential oils as title headings. Connection between ideas and images, atmosphere and narrative replay old themes of early poetry by C.S. Lewis and Ruth Pitter. Woman as all-knowing, culture as pervasive to conscience, and the gestation of healer and the healing gift as maternal are all central. The children of the womb as precious seeds of the next generation implies divine power to the unborn.

In Volume Two, "The Lion and the Unicorn" theme has historical and literary significance in both Victorian and Orwellian incarnations. The postmodern connotations of this symbolism as well as the medieval stage for both the short stories and the narrative poetry of "Castle Mount" display myth building and storytelling in various temperaments. "The Lion and the Unicorn" depicts the marriage union and in this instance relays a covenant theme. The preparation of personhood for love and home, the development of moral structure, and the resurgence of old animosity as well as the desire for revenge being transmuted into a healing gift of life-saving proportions are dominant: the hint to engage with themes that the reader will later encounter.

In "The Oracle" of Volume Two, there are thematically unified compelling word pictures and thought-provoking exploration of topics that, while they seem disparate, together form a remarkably coherent whole. Both accomplished and beautiful, the art being described and its primary characteristics have a remarkable evocation. In "Oracle of the Wild Mountain," the graduation from mythical worlds to Canadian geography makes one feel the poems are about transition and movement, so the suggestion of change and a deeper stability offered by one's roots and culture works implicitly to the theme. This section speaks of renaissance to the First

Nations of both art and spirituality by a series of altars representing various sacred animals, symbols, and persons of intrinsic value.

In Volume Three, we see the narrative between two figures—alone together, silhouetted against a background, hidden away in shadow. This is simple, lovely, and effective in bridging ostensive divides between different sections and meditations. What is later referred to as "two poets, two prophets—/Justice and Liberty/ stand in the street" in "Perestroika" becomes two voices conversing back and forth. In the last sections, depicting the seasons Spring, Summer, Autumn, and Winter respectively and named by character values, the lovers switch voices between the masculine and the feminine to convey their sentiment and betrothal to each other's ambitions and dreams.

Ideas that are prominent across the collection, in broad strokes, also provide points for discussion. First is the idea of the deified feminine, and further, of women who are fairly or unfairly persecuted as symbolic representations of a particular idea, creed, or time. Similarly, the notion of the literary heroine: we see the continual presence of Shakespeare's women in Isaacson's text, and this offers a linkage to women being woven (another recurrent metaphor) into the fabric of the nation—both the national body and its literary representations as same. Isaacson's resituating and interrogating of female figures and the purpose they serve has the implicit tie to ideas of woman as poet.

Second, the interplay between different types of worship—our veneration, frequently unquestioned, for landscape; the more programmatic veneration that takes place during a church worship service; veneration for country, themes that come out powerfully in "House of Gold" where the history of the First Nations is interwoven with a new faith, a new creed, and a new nationalism as opposed to the antinationalism, which equates to the opposite of worship.

Thirdly, in addition to different types of worship, different types of faith are discussed: personal faith in a person, an ideal or a dream is contrasted with more proscriptive types of faith, particularly organized religion and—even more particularly—Christian orthodoxy. We see in the theme a foreshadowing of the loss of a particular style of faith in the face of a new landscape upon which that faith had to be practiced.

Fourthly, the constellations, in their perpetual slate for interpretation, reinterpretation amid fixity, and their influence on the destinies of humans, play into the narrative of times when the stars, the sea, and the land were both sustenance and barriers to survival.

The inspirations for Isaacson's poetry are derived from literature, images, photographs, and nature. The poems of her childhood and teenage years through the end of university are included in "Oracle of the Stone" as a testament to the early days of her writing; one can see her progression as a poet from this point at which she first knew that to write was paramount destiny. The consequences of that choice showed her true colors as a fine character to discuss both pathos and its ramifications for the human race—when suffering is imparted for spiritual, moral, or metaphysical reasons, we also see the transformation of suffering into artwork, the harnessing of the transcendent.

This work of postmodern literature is reminiscent by virtue of its commentary on human nature and revisits Nazi Germany, examining ideas of how the British identity was shaped by the war, as well as the identity of the individual. Further, the idea of World War II and the enemy that the British fought, defined as a way of life bound by invasion and imprisonment, is once more revisited in "Glasnost." The original early manuscript of "A Wind of Morning" was submitted to W.W. Norton and was postmarked on the 60th anniversary of the liberation of Auschwitz, thus the later notation that it was dedicated to Prince William in honor of this day.

Isaacson's work, in an artistic sense, will inspire those who love authenticity. The Fleur-de-lis is a document in verse sent to Prince William over five years, beginning in 2005, which invited a yearly correspondence between them. Later, in "Libertine" bearing the titular symbol of Joan of Arc, Isaacson, through a series of soliloquy called "The Fleur-de-lis," asks to be removed from the Commonwealth of Great Britain on behalf of her country, Canada.

The Fleur-de-lis is a partaking of spiritual renaissance, defined by the cloistering and chastisement of martyrdom itself. In the text we see the richness and depth of the poet's diametrically established and ordered world. Piecing together the journey of royalty from humble beginning to glittering coronation, the poet is given to birth and pierced by nature. The language of verse speaks as medium, chronicling human nature in all its pathos and gestation.

The Emily Isaacson Institute
December 2010

INTRODUCTION

If these delicate feet could dance, the spaces would echo with tears, but the room is silent and visitors come in and out, and the windows reveal young girls outside, in imagined old leotards and ballet shoes, scuffed with time, practicing, practicing for...le danse.

The fury of the imagination is passion, and, in a stenciled, choreographed life, no movement is immaterial. Timing is exact, and the curve of your hand or the tilt of your head string a nice set of scales. When the movement is mastered, the next position demands attention and the next, like a succession of children holding hands. The creation is of the author, and passion is their forward movement.

In this book, the time that tries and the future go hand in hand. There is a responsibility to tell the truth but to veil it—through myth and symbol, through character and atmosphere, through description and abdication—so that it remains respectful of other's truths. That is the onus of poetry. The poet finds himself both master and servant, attuned to the slightest sound of nature, observer of all human nature. He seeks to attest to difference and similarity in humans, to define the road of prudence, and witness to the earth in all seasons of birth and gestation. That which nature holds in her bosom is replenished, and so the poet's words: with each new stroke of a pen, he enlivens the hearts he writes upon and finds meaning, renewing the cause of liberty.

We find richness beyond compare in deeply-felt poetic sentiment. When a reader can identify with a time, place, or person within its frame, we know that the road of literature has met us and that we have not parted ways. We can attempt to formulate our lives or imagine them into being. All things are the subject of scrutiny, reasoned with, fought with, finally brought to reason on the road of literature.

People seek out the immaculate conception in statues, scriptures, icons, and monuments, seeking the moment at which spirit becomes flesh and the spiritual nature leaves an imprint in the material world. In the field where we labor side by side, we come to perceive authenticity. There is no solace from evil except in communion. In each relevant moment, we awaken into a deeper tryst with our God-center, the immaculate conception becoming an oracle: what separates reality from what we chose as our destiny, the fantasy world from the supernatural. We are born from a heaven of miracles to an earth of poverty. Once, it was commended to speak in the tongues of men and of angels, but now it is only enough to love. In the midst of beauty and frailty, there is a quickening of hope that as the dawn we will outdo the night and speak.

This response requires courage and dignity, bravery, and the chastisement that brings peace. In all things, may there be peace, and in the divine warrior, there is no blood tide, no crimson conflict, no jaded response. There is clarity and purpose and truth. There is a method to renounce what brings fear and embrace what causes love. We will be the victor in the end, of the simple life and bridled pathos.

Humanity is the natural flower of love. Without it the emotion and pathos of mankind would not exist. The poetry of ages past claims God and gods as both supernatural and glorious, capable of imparting their qualities and assets to humans on earth. It induces a liturgical framework for both song and the written word; it abdicates attention from the minute to the larger scale. In the beginning, the world was dark; now, with poetry, it is lit, although dimly. The poets' words transcend the dark ignorance of mankind. We are all waiting to be illumined, warned, caught in the throes of innocence, tamed. For a future happiness, we delay gratification, wait for a somber yield, the structure of planting and harvest. For the present, we hope for a renunciation of suffering, of poverty, of illness.

When I first discovered the poetry of C.S. Lewis and Ruth Pitter's biography, Hunting The Unicorn, I had no idea that I would be the privileged sharer of a figurative relationship between two poets that entailed the Oxford cloak all of Lewis spiwery, his thoughts, her ideas: of the chartering of freedom after a war, the imagination of a poet, of story's legacy, of a bloodied people. Looking back from the other side of prolific skill with such destiny, of aloneness echoing the fury of gods, from the stilted movements of a few last composers against the night; God in all three persons resounded like a hunting horn, and we were the hunted.

> I will not cease from mental fight,/ Nor shall my sword sleep in my hand/ Till we have built Jerusalem/ In England's green and pleasant land.
>
> —William Blake

We are taming the oracle of our years, of distance and of silence. We have constructed a play, and when we stand to give our soliloquy, we will see again the matchless heaven, the sounding board earth, and the view from the shadows.

I opened the arms of my soul and embraced the world.

—Emily Isaacson

THE LAUREL WREATH

THE DOOR

THE DOOR
gallery

The eight projections,
each with a coat of arms:
one for the dominion
and one for each of the
seven provinces
to enter Confederation...
Prince Edward Island,
the last, in 1873.
The gallery floors
were originally
covered with
plate glass
an inch thick,
to allow the maximum
possible penetration
of light
from above.
The interior woodwork
of the library was
contracted to
Israel Page.
The paneling
are elaborately
carved in white pine from
the Ottawa valley.

entrance

The gothic entrance door,
connecting the library
with the Houses
of Parliament,
displays deeply
incised figures
of Canadian wild animals
including
mink, fox, beaver,
raccoon, heron, and eagle.

reception

Ash, oak, cherry, and walnut—
all native woods—
form the rich
parquetry floor.

The parliamentary
complex
was formally opened
with a grand ball held by
the Governor General,
Lord Dufferin.
Carriage
after carriage arrived
on the spring evening of
March 27, 1876,
and fifteen hundred guests,
gaily appareled in costumes
of every imaginable sort
were received.

isis

The eight projections
of the human soul:
to transcribe the brilliant,
to extrapolate the noble,
to elucidate the prized,
to memorize the noteworthy,
to extract the pure,
to conceptualize the abstract,
to go into exile,
to fight for one's liberty.

FRANCE

PARIS

PARIS. Le Dome de l'Hotel des Invalides

Where angels shine my floor
squaring against one another
in the dust, seraphıms poor,
squatting to receive: blind,
in the
apples of my eyes—

Flowers in the mist,
the grapes of such smooth gold,
un sauvignon blanc
that trellised time could last forget;
the patterned gait of St. Soldier's Square,
un Jardin de la Princesse, and
last minute wanderings
and whisperings
amongst the graves.

PARIS. *Sacré-Coeur de Montmartre*

Under the piano,
rifling through
La Pathétique in sepia,
the rust of
my head, oiled, rests
cross-stitched in fertility:
Queen Anne's lace, blanched,
weathered on the crest
like the virgin shore
of white sand dunes...

Spring,
the garden tapestry
of my child:
like thread,
supple
and wound,
black to red
elaborated in its time;
purity in
one line:
with seven sets of
bedsheets—
orchids,
sphere to column,
wine-white.

Maison de la Liberté

In spring,
waves that grace the sea,
a simmered adagio,
antique judgments
like a painter's oil;
camphor, an aid
to digestion,
glittering on the
burgundy dark cobblestones:
the horses, gelding and bay,
shining in the rain.

An innocent girl,
under a noble hymn
rides into battle:
before the angels Gabriel
and Michael, a virgin laurel
gracing a fair, chaste maiden,
her flag bearing
the fleur-de-lis
beneath the gold and hues
of morning.

Our Lady of
the Northern Crown:
still echoing across
the sky,
across the night,
across the sea,
across Orléans,
across the pastoral countryside,
peace.

HOUSE OF GOLD

HOUSE OF GOLD
House of Gold

The old house sat in the shadows,
weathering the seasons
and footprints through the garden.

Casting art upon its walls
making a sanctuary of origins
and watercolor night.

The totem lay under a covering:
in its face
was carved
an eagle,
a mother,
a moon.

The First Nations' artisans
carved it from cedar,
a gift
to our city
and sister city
Oyama, Japan.

The train continued on its way
through meadow and mountain,
its steam pilfering into the open sky
and the moon patterned
the fields like chintz.

Linen Medium

She sat in a small room,
stroking the canvas
into song,
waiting until
her audience
burst into laughter or tears.

How intelligent you are,
she thought
to notice this primeval impulse
to act like gods
in a small room.

I shall hang each painting
in a gallery
in a small town,
in a small room.

They clapped in the auditorium
at how she bowed beneath the weight
of years
and honed the impulse
to dance like the gods,
painting angels,
blue and white lights aflicker,
in a small room.

True Patriot Love

Canada,
a virgin woodland
so rebirthed
emboldened,
countenance unfeigned
after two thousand years,
solemn and sacred—
the cross of jeweled stones
in a monastery
of unchartered
martyrdom
and liturgy.

The Loom of the North

Something is always
simmering on the black stove
and in the journal of time;
she wrote of
the shining northern purity
of a female icon—
love and sincerity
in the figurative,
stargazing in the field,
weeping at transgression:
the sorrow of her eyes,
the sweetness of her mouth—

Stretched on a loom,
the huge white cloth
of the North;
we were the threads,
short and long,
our ways
stretched across it.

Mica

In the beginning,
there was the legend,
whispering in the cold;
the trade began,
one drum of oil,
one vat of wine,
one keg of brewed beer,
one barrel of apples,
one sack of potatoes,
one quart of water,
one pound of flour,
and the story went on—
the sky birthed us in pain,
one Mona Lisa,
wrapped
in a fur.

Before The Rain

In the silence
that stills the field,
at day's end
the promise of harvest,
a diadem to the poor:
sitting on the ground
in the dirt
soothing the fear
of hunger,
the tragedy of little—
the gold
beneath the might,
and the worship
of a creator,
berries of purple,
a tragedian
of royalty.

Origins

In a western
once-promised land,
litany composed
from the French and Latin,
flawless,
filtering root indifference;
softening our static,
straight edges around the moon
modern,
compromised sky-song,
flowing and reshaping
our incantations of
earlier life forms.

Wilderness

In the dry hills,
lisped and forgotten;
sandy, and breathing
in rhythm,
a virgin forest
with biting cold
and feathery branches—
each night a gently
sloping gold:
the suitor of the sun
in full splendor,
the stars of
aspen night,
piercing the darkness
one by one,
and lullaby
soft-dreamed,
still—
downriver,
downwind,
a life of one's worth,
a thousand miles
into the wilderness
of soul.

Man of Sorrows

The face was not cold,
like expensive white marble,
but lonely,
discomforting with
a wider, deeper
acceptance of the north sun:
orange, and
alluring.

He hung with hands
outstretched
in a cold cathedral,
subdued martyrdom
latent in the echoes
of the ornate gold throne.

Familiar with anguish,
the tapestry hangs on the wall:
millions of gilt gold threads
and singular purity,
the face of a madonna
with child.

Monastery

Undertones
of pine and moss
in the mild air,
the garden scent of wildflowers,
the pathways
leading to the river lookout.

A sanctuary of
stained glass:
the light through
shadows streaming,
the Saint,
beautiful and true—
the pipe organ,
an idyll
behind a warm welcome;
twenty-two monks
listening for
a Bach
prelude and fugue.

White Crosses

At the crosses left
on city streets,
one small flower from
my pocket:
sometimes
I stand snow-broken
on the edge
of a road—
as they,
untouched,
fade, mark
the exact ordinary
place where loss
occurred;
beloved graves
covered with
snow white
hyacinths
and
small white
stones.

HOUSE OF THE SNOW

House of the Snow

Canadian winter
flew down on the wings of an owl,
submerged a small settlement
in a blanket of snow:
riveted by icicles frozen
from the rooftops,
where fires blazed
in the hearth,
green and red holly
and cedar bracken
graced the mantelpiece.

The snowflakes,
silver
poignant and sure,
measured in time to
drifts of white
where footprints
were unique,
one by one
subdued
deep
and dreaming
in snow.

Snow Angels

On the wooden sidewalk
covered in snow,
horses making
tracks in
metal shoes,
bumpy over the still
terrain, pewter—
the light in the distance
blown
into fiery
subterfuge,
each silence
and shout,
a refuge
against
our cool
calm
collected
night.

Starboard

Sea-salt hair,
traipsed in the wind,
we journeyed 91 days
amid the steamer trunks—
this is my account
of the voyage at sea:
white salt caked to
the yellow moon,
rounded and full,
like the rind of a lemon,
one moment estranging
another, your
storm-shaped rhythm
pointing a clear trail
through the night sky,
cloaked
in great bears
and gentle footsteps;
blurred into
the soft and blue,
porpoises crossed
our trails,
silvery gray.

New World

The ships set sail for the New World,
landing on a new shore,
lighting a sacred fire.

The nuns
in black and white habit,
bent in prayer,
teaching lessons
one at a time,
dispersing the knowledge
to a new land.

St. Mary's of the
Immaculate Conception
housed the native children of
British Columbia,
providing a school in the
mountains of the sun,
braving the elements,
directing the minds
of the young and innocent
toward an eternal plight.

Candlelit Portrait

Native people,
with strong bones,
full rosebud lips,
and wide
stargazing
almond eyes,
living in the
fiery
stained glass
windows
of the
Immaculate
Conception
Church:
the laughter
of sons
glancing in the rafters
like turtledoves.

Bark Tea

We boiled the bark
in hot water
over the fire,
stripping it from the trees
with reluctance
albeit
tender obedience
to nature and its laws.

A remedy for sailors,
who have traveled the seas
and taken ill.

To care in a moment
for the prevention
is a cure:
first do no harm.

Seascape

White-rimmed,
created for
conception
of respite
into beautiful—
provocatively familiar,
crashing against
the Mirandean shore,
into the
autumn,
rich
in the innocence
of the inspirational
world.

Orion

A dreamer of the North,
of wind, of fire, and of water,
like a lodge overgrown
with moss,
behind the northern lights,
beyond a wall of mist:
his footsteps
walking down,
his walking stick, aligned,
to see the bears cross the sky,
to see the ladle of the stars;
like night sounds,
slow across the
path,
sun-steadied,
about to fall...
they give themselves
to his arrows.

Indian Mosaic

Stills
meadows
to dew,
breathes through
sacred tundra,
rivets the forest
under the
full moon,
lights
fire
to crimson.

Unearthed
clams and
mussels,
steam-baked
slow
over the
beach rocks...

And stars
to burn
the sky.

River Cabin

North as a place
in the mind
where a safe house
coexists
with a much-needed
wilderness.

Blackcap and
red huckleberry,
nettle and fern,
cascara, buttercup,
burnished hazelnut,
and red rose hips.

Peppergrass,
Indian plum
in an open wood,
dandelion suns dotting
the wild grass,
and coltsfoot,
inhabiting the shaded ground
of the river bank.

The trailing blackberry
wound its way
along the neck
of the forest;
its purple-seeded harvest
a steeped nectar
over the fire.

Immaculate

O Immaculate,
the blood of thy soul
salutes thee,
the lambs
before thee:
the restitutional
world
exhibits thee,
the reservoir of thy
hope attends thee;
the castile moon
over the
water,
dormant
pale,
a child
smoothed
from the
sky
of heaven.

HOUSE OF THE SEA
House of the Sea

———

Queen Charlotte,
an island on the far side
of night;
constellation of stars and
mouth of the sea,
a table of plenty
beneath the harvest of moon.

The veiled echo of
England's famed cathedral:
of waves and wind,
of night sky and distant land...
to no longer hear
the sound
of the storm.

Amaryllis

Embedded in winter-quiet earth,
purified by the layers of time,
a bulb dormant until the moment
of birth,
then sighing its way into view,
unlike
the crests of mountains,
of ocean and shore,
of the pale green color
that meant life;
and I: a seed
in safe shelter,
hiding beneath the soil,
waiting for the moment
of rebirth,
cloistered at the edge
of the forest.

Liturgy

Song-chained flutters,
for words of
house or home,
Jerusalem's temple doves,
in dedication
to exile
form allegiance;
their litany,
moving the water
next to the still
solid earth:
faintly salted,
to shelter
and contain it.

Shore

The imagined mirror
of time and plenty
where the green waters
gave forth a harvest
to last the winter.

The driftwood
peopled the shore
and surf pounded
a breaking rhythm.

To walk the sands
of time,
both past and future:
to find the eternal song.

Legend carried us far,
an island tapered
by wild winds
and wildflowers.

Dawn

Constellations
in the pale light
over the tundra,
the tall grass in the meadow,
winking
at the coming
morning...

My garden grows
undisturbed,
thyme, rosemary,
and marjoram
unblighted,
inclined,
brightened with
the flowers
of indigo petals and
yellow goldenrod;
a silent prayer
upon the altar
of peace.

Portrait

At a high point,
I rode for three
miles, unhindered,
through the thrush altars
and golden grass,
the eucalyptus-hued
silhouette
like a small, undated
black and white
photograph:
over the Saskatchewan
fields of rye,
into the distance
on an old black mare.

Three Sisters Stew

Saint Augustine
in all of twenty-two rows
grew corn and beans,
squash and savory;
like mist over the plains,
their Three Sisters Stew
a staple of the North,
and Indian stature
of wombs with eyes
to gaze into the
heart of the earthly and
divine:
each child
a new planet
into the constellation
of sun, wind, and tears.

New Moon

The watercolors
of the Arctic Inuit
bloom round
the cabin door,
a stream to cloak the
Northern star,
nursed in a pine cone.

And the moon was
round and full,
a silent song in a dusty sky
filled with regret and longing,
each night the close
to a gold-rimmed dream.

What we thought of Creator,
maker of the earth
and singer of the ancient song,
was a liturgy of legend
drummed in solemn chants.

We turned the pages of time,
and the fire burned,
the ground was
turned under
and the prayers
like seeds
beneath the earth
grew into a field,
row upon row:
became our sustenance.

The Fleur-de-lis

Her
first child
of the morning,
in procession,
under oath,
a pilgrim
to Our Lady,
promising to go
hither to
Notre Dame, if God give
him the grace to return.

We mounted the steed
under the banner of the fleur-de-lis
and rode into battle.

The troops acquiesced,
and the English surrendered,
freeing the throne.

The lovely peasant was
imprisoned a martyr,
legend made her a revolutionary,
history proclaimed her a saint.

Star of the Sea Art Gallery

Trembling aspens
rooted among the moss
and ferns,
the white-tailed deer,
elk and bear,
silent like the ethereal
white sun,
the boron of
Saskatoon bushes,
a Pleiades and Orion
to the solar
constellation
of immaculate
childhood:
sea stars left on an
old arctic bench.

Wedding Wreath

Sure as the leaves have turned to gold,
and light's last whisper, fading,
the pathway through the northern wood,
espoused winter's adoration.

Fragrant doe, the forest speaks,
its gale a humble treatise,
the footprints leveled through the snow,
the glass of our baptisement.

'Midst cedar shoots and nettle bracken,
St. John's wort and calendula flow'rs,
lily of the valley, our sole chastisement,
through summer's gold and winter's cold,
it's I will walk with you.

HOUSE OF THE ROSE
House of the Rose

———

The wild carrot flower
grew in the royal garden,
and the Lady of Denmark,
consort to the king,
was an expert lace maker.

She challenged the court ladies
to create their best lace,
in the fine and dainty
fashion of the garden flower,
antique white.

No one could rival
the Queen Anne's handiwork,
so fair and lovely
was her pattern: as the white
florets of her lace collar.

As the legend says,
she pricked her finger
and a single drop of blood
fell in the center, coloring it purple,
and so it remains to this day.

Winter Tryst

He set
the queenly figure
of a woman
into the branches
of a tree
in the snow-thickened
forest
that nearly enclosed her;
the woman in the tree
was not surprised
by the strange
cold land...
she regarded
him in the forest
as a man kneeling
before her
in an icy
cold
diamond.

The Incarnation of Troy

She was carved in wood,
like wind:
holy, haloed,
still as the sacred ground;
a miracle of harvest embedded
in her scarred hands,
budding spruce in the shade,
flourishing in the wet stone,
the heroine
stately as beautiful mares
on the plains of Troy.

Dyes

The indigo of night
for your dress,
the forest table of my eternal repast
in the Great Hunting Ground,
the goldenrod yellow
of summer,
salmon-red fringes
of my buckskin coat,
and arrowheads
to hunt the bear and elk
forged in a fire
at the door of my tipi.

Native Land

From the north chamber,
shining, you would see the moon,
the ocean we would inherit—
still and quiet;
and over the sea,
the seven mountain ranges,
one with oil,
sweeter than the others,
one with honey,
fruit hung heavy,
one with milk.

Incantation of Harvest

Water, wind, earth, and sky,
spring, autumn, summer, winter;
the wildflowers of our landscape,
gourds, cream, and pine
are plowed like Celtic rainsongs
into the fields;
unburned, our heritage
like fine wine ages—
kept in a cask
for each next generation.

Then the Great Spirit
breathed from the North
of the divine,
of wilder devotion
to the virgin account;
we collected the columbines:
seashells along the trails
of the shore,
and nothing was wasted.

Log House

A refuge for the besieged,
a pure sanctuary,
and a ceremonious
cover of a man's
instinct to
sustain life by fending
off winter,
nursing one,
like a child
under the deep purpose
of mercy.

The North Wind

Two gold wedding rings,
buried, engraved,
beneath the cedar tree,
its roots massive
and solid to earth.

The soil, home to the fern
and buttercup
in a vale of
open space.

The deer
eat the daisies,
leaving cloven tracks
in the soft dew.

The wind
sweeps the stream
into the valley,
rippling the crystal
smooth surface,
soothing the
parched land,
waiting for a salute
from the North—
of hail and snow,
the winter's vast
garment of white.

Store

I donned a flowered
apron once,
under the shelves of
French linen,
eiderdown-cream,
currant pie and ham,
bins and English china,
spiced hot-cross-buns,
dolls and blue lollipops,
red oats, rye, and whiskey,
cornish game hens and
flour for the rolling pin.

Priest

Under the cross,
Latin filtering the light
through the trees;
Japanese maple,
russet,
midnight in the
falling gold:
black cloaks
wavering
through the smoky haze,
taize, like incense,
rippling the sky.

Naveed

With sun above and earth below
the guardian of a single star
that rumples night with steady glow
streams heaven to the ocean floor.

Her halo shines for all to hear
the words of light to mankind's tear,
her chore of alteration to our best,
winsome as the last request.

She stands, the token of dawn's first grace,
inviting the peoples of native lands to taste
a feast set out in rich repast, wine and bread,
a table of fiery silver and damask rose-red.

The marriage of a manhood in its prime,
to love beyond the veil of silken time;
to ne'er forget the moment of truth,
the upbringing of covenant
and chance of truce.

HOUSE OF THE RIVER'S BEGINNING

House of the River's Beginning

Under the
hawthorn quilt,
there is somewhere
a river
into the night.

Fast and bright,
echoing in
the nave:
highland song
carried, pure
and even,
kneeling
like a boy choir
on the
wind of Gregorian
hymn.

Homestead

A sailboat mosaic
in amber glass,
sectioned
for each wave,
each sun,
each cloud,
cut green, blue, yellow,
silver sailing on
past the kitchen
window.

Another Damask Road

Soft, salt-whitened,
along the shore
in the evening,
the cold like coals
flecked
from the sea:
the danger of
purity and solace
in the dark gray foam,
the solemn dunes and
flower lace melding out
in a vale behind
the wood-roped
road,
your stars,
blinking
to
each crest
of hill.

School Room

A peaceable rule
in my classroom
does not omit
the shuffling of papers,
the swinging of doors,
the slow whistles,
and the resonant structure
of the poem.

They sat in the rows
of wooden desks
holding a canticle of order,
the white cliffs far away
estranging us through
silent epiphany
like a white widow,
haloed over the sea.

In the stillness,
everything is desert and oasis,
the wanting a reverent
and punctual time,
that would take the hands of Israel
like a queen.

Old Man River

The rain shape-shifted
on the star-watching rock,
inoperable
beside the grail reeds,
the fish like
the scaled
hourglass,
turning and turning,
fishermen, waist-deep
in the dreams
of lye:
in fields,
hands outstretched
just beyond
the moon.

Plains Indians

Handpicked for
the sacred ritual,
the spring buffalo rite:
one dance,
masked in their
paint;
fires of midnight
cloistering the plains,
the morning rising
among the ashes of
footprints
and feathers.

Progeny

The spring came and melted
the mountain snow:
flowing down
in rushing streams—
your smile,
saturated
with tears
to fill a bottle—
dripping from the branches;
and opaque sunset,
your vine press
ripening azure
to dusk
under the watchful
eye
of sons
to outnumber
the corseted
stars.

Rockies

Stretched over the horizon
from a stone hunch,
a formidable cloak of gray
and insurmountable
face of time,
the mountains
congeal the rain into snow
and ice,
making the mortal
hemisphere feel
the pain of cold and
still,
swift
hunger.

Risen from the death
under a mantle of white,
the cliffs loom
precariously,
touching sun's
first light.

Spring

Queen Anne,
lace of the crown,
unabridged;
gold cord of light,
and warmth
descending, lark,
into a dark
fairyland
deep in the earth—
the place from which
seed,
fragile and stark,
begins
its journey
into eternity.

The Madonna

An oracle:
now the sea
will be wild,
pushing at her pursuers
to dance the
floundering boat,
whales away,
before she strokes in
her breath—
created, preserved,
and undestroyed.

Harbor

Until daylight,
pouring out
of the sky,
silver, the varnish
on a crown,
icy with winter's stealth,
gown of sapphires and velvet,
the head of saffron gold
decried a fury
of pointed colloquialism—
isles away in
Victoria Bay,
erecting
a figurehead
monument
in wax.

HOUSE OF THE PHYSICIAN

House of the Physician

Wandering on a lonely shore,
feet draped with the sand-salt—
God in light,
jarred from the night
out of heaven;
God beside us,
God before us,
God within us,
surrounding us,
impermeable,
impenetrable,
immortal,
invisible.

Magnolia at Dusk

Statuesque and
ocean-born,
bright,
the hue of nectar
to gods and kings,
still stately
in bronze,
a medal in
unmerciful weather;
under the heavens,
growing
resplendent and sacred:
at sundown,
a patient of virtue,
outside the old house
of the doctor.

One Blue Candle

She used to be quiet Catholic,
St. Christopher's medals, and
one blue candle,
lit for you
in a cathedral,
of stained-glass and stone;
the Montreux school
in the old mansion,
always filled with new flowers
and quiet conversation...

Now she endures
being told
by a cold court
that the pyramid
of art, medicine, and science
does not uphold
the compassionate viewpoint,
the ministering hand to guide,
the victory to another
life without such sorrow.

We wait—
a thousand in line—
for a fountain in a rock,
while Jerusalem's wailing wall
is stuffed with prayers.

Envision

Stars strung bold with
purpose, like hymns,
unplayed—
resilient,
attending their
authors.

Light by light,
their notes
in castle
shining;
by dawn
held fast,
a scepter
to the gold.

Holy Land

In a new frontier:
leafy
with olive,
the ponies
cross the vast lands
just before dark...
brushing against
your skin,
ivory,
long nights into the
wilderness...
stars against
our fiery hearts, strung;
like Plato—
citrus-yellow
in the plantations—
years of honor
in a promised land,
dripping
with pears and
goat's milk.

Constellation

We are as flowering dogwood
and Nootka rose,
planets moving
through the night
lens of milky universe,
transient as the seasons pass
without appeasement,
at the mercy of the storm.

Yet now,
I have completed
a measurable act:
I have built a home
in the wilderness,
where the beams,
warm with the smoke
of a hearth-fire,
are hung with elk
and bear,
dried sorrel and madrona;
maize and beans
dot the soup
with gold stars
in the spring sky.

Bridle Of The North

In the reach of
St. Roch,
expect equilibrium:
two tunes,
strung
rhapsody—
true North,
true love—
under the twilight
of the
northern star.

The dance of
summer and winter,
the marriage of
spring and fall,
bringing forth
children
after a dream,
to equate
love and eternity.

Inside The Hill

Knarled,
one small iris
on the wings of angels
planted itself
in the crook
of my branches;
naiads and dryads
took a fancy to
your closet
finery,
silks and
velvets,
ropes of pearls.

Window Prism

Solace in the home
flows and rises
to surface,
indifferent of its peace—
moments scarred
in the incompleteness;
our gifts of love and mercy,
moving color to
higher ground.

The rainbow
streaked across
the wall;
pupils dilated with
harmony,
and the night
became day,
by the watercolor
stroke of summer.

Chartres Cathedral

Kneeling in the cold
block,
head bowed
at the prayers
of martyrdom,
long hair,
red as the field
beside the island river;
a tapestry in orchid,
a trust
as basic as David,
an old blessing,
a threefold tent;
the night, deep as the shadows,
like an abyss, drew my bodice once,
and my blood ran cold—
but the door had been barred forever
and I held fast,
weeping at the
door.

O Immortal

Immortal God,
ever-present
crucifix:
be innocent of my blood;
omnipotent,
invisible,
the wind
round about us,
cloistering us,
inhabiting
the shores
of our nation,
indivisible.

ODE TO ENCHANTMENT

BATTERSEA BRIDGE
Battersea Bridge

In the middle,
cold and the wind,
howling
over the
parapet,
dark and
lifeless,
broken into
a crumpling
of dreams,
about to
consume despair
or gratitude.

Laughter at Oxford

One late
afternoon, poet
sanding away
at a nobler journey,
leaves drifting
into later pools
that drip
with years,
of bare wood
floors, mute …

One bench sings
with stolen youth:
romance, hushed,
staring out
under the cascade
of gentleness.

To An Aged Don

Dear sir,
from "The Taste of
Pineapple: A Basis for Literary
Criticism,"
your "emphasis
on the quiddity
of things"
sustains your star-darts
in the heavens
as we wait for
the Most Holy
Sacrament,
buoyant
upon the flames
of civilization.

Of a War

Staring down the
gallows,
barrels of clouds,
rifling on the
horizon
into the next
lesson of mankind's
brutal frame:
the floating of
conception
(steeped in glory):
a charge and banner.

Crown of Thorns

You who consumed
all humanity's
brokenness
in one crushed
cross—
a crown of thorns
yet perched
on the brow
of a Jewish carpenter;
simple are your
currents, blowing
against the night,
against the star-splattered
sky.

Meditations in a Flame

Captive to my
merchants
in the eye of the
aurora,
eclipsed into eternity—
warers and vendors,
stumbling over
the dogs,
skewed among the flames;
each fruit, from a blossom,
each having torn a leaf.

O cross of thorns:
how desperate is your
eye, unseen,
in the voice of his dying.

Eye of the Storm

Crucified
in deep suspicion,
the wreck
harbored deep
beneath the gold.
In squalid liberty,
we candidly
renounce
(beneath the rancor),
your deep black and
white
criticism.

Quill and Ink

Under witticism,
rifling through
old
pages,
charitable with poetic
intent,
the flower garden watered
and green
with honor, incense,
insight, wonders, terrors
of a poet's soul...

Overhead,
the roses,
translucent-white
to crown you—
the verse so sweet
with summer, rung
over the hills
of down.

In Prison

The magical impulse,
architectured
in latent
realms,
solaced by
cement—
we dance,
inebriated at the
bare bars of
hell's gate—
aching for nothing,
walking the floors
white as lead,
like tulips buried
beneath the snow:
the moon,
a madonna.

Emeritus

On a platform,
smocked,
daintily sketching
your wildflower
haloes and prism
eyes—
cornflower blue,
ceramic sky
falling out of
heaven and Atlantis.

Shepherds,
we encircle
our flock,
devoid of the
six eyes
of a cherubim's wing:
flattered and frail.

Walk Amongst the Shrines

Gravestones,
heaped with rubble—
all our transcendent
incantations
steeped
over the fires,
mourning the
ethereal night-green
boy
burning
charcoal against the
fragile, lost.

THE RIVER

The River

Westward
on the floats,
winding downriver
transpired
under the nets
of dark-haired women.

The train floats by,
its trestle rain-shook
and wintery;
the mosaic of
water-bright
fish eyes,
giddy
among the wild grass.

Where the moon
is harnessed under
the sky,
over the white
slat-board church,
a eunuch
carries his mother,
still bright,
like a lotus
blooming
under the bile sun.

Farm Boy

Taking the pickaxe
to a pile of wood
for one day of
November, the cold
and frost
icing the tree limbs,
firewood piled in the
foyer.

Swinging the
bucket,
lashing from the pump
one morning's worth
of tea:
our herbs
in all flavors,
we fall into the pansies,
too simple for a bath.

Chronicle

Under
the shadows
of old bookstore dust,
shaded and bleary-eyed,
having drunk
an ounce of ruby tea
in an old stone cup;
your velvet cape,
an eloquent verse,
the gallows,
stacks reaching into
thin air—
their ebullient glory,
a page leaf.

Folds of a flapper's
dress, still
sequined, between
the tissue
in an
olive wood chest.

Caravan

One thatched roof,
a sprinkling of
firs into the forest,
gypsies
light their terra-cotta
lanterns
in vibrant hue,
gold glittering in the
salty dust,
among the peasant feet,
worn,
washed in the basins
of the world.

Bombs and Gallows

In the mountains of the sun,
camped in the open field,
the moon was fiery red...

Looking up in the night,
at a million eyes
whistling in the darkness,
cows braying at the smoke,
the river's song in pewter,
the grass, like garlands;
still, in the dampened reeds
of Gabriel's grace.

The shattering of
black hail,
into the nestling of
wild roses,
oboes screeching
in the decks, your lacy
fingers at our throats—
we laid the cards,
black queen, black heart,
one club, one spade,
for a game of parlor.

Draped in wine,
we cross the sky,
flourish through the night,
and mark our
marble epitaphs.

Shetland Pony

The country:
blueberry wine,
white and blue
china on the
vine-encroached table,
hyacinths streaked
with water,
cream-colored
cloths layered
under the peasant feast;
wood-lacquered baskets
blooming,
in navy and
petal-white.

Winding
out beneath us,
the roads that
disappear...
we go on,
the horses trotting,
on and on;
the lights
in the distance,
soft noses, in velvet,
on and on.

Gold Vermilion

Ethan,
ever after referred
to as an open-ended
conversationalist,
heavy-witted,
sold on a prospect,
like a fine gladiator
swinging a heavy sword,
amid the nursery-tale
treasury in Flan.

Straight-edged silver
with long curls
reaching to his
sword-hilt,
swung for battle;
horses
in the Parthenon,
striped,
blue and gold,
and liqueur,
like chocolate
brandy.

Dante

In the still
mist world,
the inner chambers
of the
moon unworn,
inlaid with
clarity, smoked—
ringless
in your stormy eyes,
one unicorn
leaps from
the falls ...

Nuns chanting,
haunting
the fall,
the early autumn,
paisley:
one olive tree
in plain song,
plaited hair
bound
with ribbons.

Motet

Dryads melting into
infernos, deaf
with self-pity, caked in
pig's manure,
vile with rage;
streaming with blood,
the sylphs, a silent
movement, white and black
ravens and pawns
draped in flour sacks,
the silver cuff links
in the library.

Clutching a wire
harem, veering
to the left, esteemed
delphinium,
like pumpernickel
in a cool,
dark closet
with the dead-of-night
rats.

Valentine Raptures

The red door
swung open,
unsuspecting
of the left-handed
visitor,
crocheted squares like
the breezes ...

In hearts and roses,
willowing
our tresses
into love-knots.

Ballet

The night drew a silent line
in the theatre against
the thunderous audience,
the orchestra paused in the pit,
the violin's resonant soprano
an elite comprehension,
and the conductor metered
the seconds.

The dance hung on
the verge
of worlds;
each adagio, the measure
of a moment
with or without beauty's resin
and the demarcation
of mystique.

The crinoline swished
with toe shoes en pointe,
en pirouette
across the floor rubbed
a solemn pattern—
arabesque, the nightingale
of soft-spoken moments,
and a choreographed
future to mimic poise.

THE POET

The Poet

___

In panes,
under the candles of the sky,
ladled like soup to the common
and poor, who
adrift—
rage their dreams
and sonnets
crease the night.

Back from the death,
all story spiwery,
hangs
its cloak,
wick in its covering
by the fire,
the beautiful,
cradled
in her peace.

The Bread

Leavened,
the oven parches
and prepares
the sacred loaf to
dry perfection.

Piece by piece, torn
into white segments,
to participate with
wine
in sorrow and suffering,
in forgiveness and repentance—

And rebirth,
knowing our hostile hearts
he came,
and the direction of his love
is an endless
source, repeating the grace
of a moment in time,
forever.

Acacia

One pearl
among the blackberry
leaves, amid
pine and field—
African lace
blowing in the whitened
breeze,
over the clank
of steel.

Three children play
under the
tangle-wood bed
and the yellow
halls
resound
with whales and
cabbages
underfoot.

The garden of arugula,
downwind;
laughter
and I
part shaded,
amongst the
mornings.

Pale Lights

One moon,
reflected in
a shallow pool,
like a seashell
in a foreign sky,
azure,
her skirts swirled,
garnet
under the night—
her silk like
corn, burnished
over coals,
and water,
too pure
to drink.

Old Worlds

Crocus under
the magnolia,
spotted white and gold,
gentle lions
cross my path,
pawing and roaring,
the sun falling out
of heaven
into the sepulchral orbit
of gentle kings
and strong queens,
reminiscent
of the river's mouth,
and an orchard
by the ruins
of an old castle.

Other Suns

In the seventh
constellation
of the milky way,
Neptune,
through a sword,
brandished in jest,
Jupiter,
jumping in
and out of well pools,
Saturn,
spell-deep:
Earth,
resilient and verdant,
Venus,
resplendent
as wildflowers
over Olympia,
Mars,
salient as
breaking oceans' roar,
Uranus's eagles
swift
in eventide,
Pluto,
a simple salutation,
and Mercury-white coals,
a thousand years
into the dawn.

Other Galaxies

On the garden
bench,
the auburn head
bent over the violin,
sun-glazed
skirts, fading
navy and lilac
in the shadows;
the melon balls on plates,
the shawls of lace,
memories like tulle
around the
miniature horses.

Crushed ice
and a maraschino cherry—
you had one good hat,
and wore it
with a jaunt;
your coat,
combed black wool,
your dark hair
hidden under
a lacquer of fortes.

Peacocks
strutting
over the lawn:
little cherubs
in the terraced gardens,
running down to
the stream's pale
violet haunt.

Chrysanthemum

Glowing hot coffee,
your eyes,
walking on coals,
drinking
your
cream, crushed
from vine-ripened
destiny.

From the white sea,
sand-dollars deep
on the deep bottom
of clarity,
where my feet
touch
you gently,
gently touch you,
our seahorses,
dried and brittle.

Stone Fortress

One summer's night,
the old library,
mahogany,
emerald light
at dusk
mapping the long tables
of silent students—

Studying
the water carrier,
the ram, the eagle,
the unicorn, the serpent,
the dove, the wolf,
the centaur, the whale
under a handful
of stars, sacred and
rock-silent in a cradle—

Each constellation's lullaby
re-seeding the fields
of night, with fixity
a counterpoint
to variable destiny.

The moon, a wide mouth,
swallowing
the seas of darkness.

Hearth Fire

In the cold, smooth North,
under the sharp ring of
winter solstice,
knee-deep in novels,
four children deep
in dreams,
like monks in books,
we pull them from the world's
seashells, unbroken—

Willow tree ornaments
shored like driftwood
on the mantle, each
one an elusive olive-skinned
vagabond.

Shining Armor

Arms crossed
on the old wooden bench;
hair, lithe
in a breeze.

Summer-browned,
with curled skins
in pools
around your ankles,
pared for pie;
the apple tree,
a hearty son at dusk,
the soft-wood
house ruffled
like eyelet
amongst the trees...
a sonatina child,
its shining
whisperer.

A WIND OF MORNING

HALO OF THE NIGHTINGALE

Iris

Intricacies of a thousand buds,
diamonds shimmering in the grass,
wept the fragile night
of spring,
held back, torn
asunder,
like a nightingale
dances
with the moon;
nameless, still,
how the pale
rests in purple cloaks
of reticent color:
epiphany in the
seed, still unchanging
for
a thousand glass
years of gold.

Enter.

HALO OF TIME

Chronos

Pewter-still lake,
mirroring
each equal drop,
a meteor
into your dawn.

Each fragile note,
an equal sun,
an uncreased garment,
equatoring the noons
of heaven.

Kairos

The world
was given to birth:
mother
and daughter,
flourishing
under the pear
tree, dew
lighting their heads
to chord,
fragrant
like a crown.

HALO OF ALABASTER

Forest

Clear and crystal,
sweet over the moss...

And tree banks,
whispering
joy music
over the olive.

To the sky,
anew, I taste
cedar leafy spice:
holy water.

Garden

Brief
unspoken angel
wraps the sky in
spiels of color;
under the pathways,
bulbs
hibernate
in winter caskets,
alabaster souls
wrinkling in the
eyes of God.

Notation

Chiseled
dream note:

moon yellow
under
the boughs, listen
to the unicorns—
bright
and beautiful,
bold and free,
swinging their tails
to the rhythm
of hooves, crashing
through the vales
under the pale,
steadfast
like silver.

HALO OF ORION

Little Dipper

At dawn,
the stars fly
out in
progression...

One by one
to the
horizon;
golden-silver
still
holding each other's
hands,
lest
one should
fall
back,
too transparent,
into the silent
night.

Saturn

Simple,
bright stark-birthed,
in unseeing focus
and love pierced cry:
as angel's wings,
all humanity shivers,
feather-like,
frail;
our once-cradled
dust
floating,
candlelit
toward
the silence
of heaven.

Neptune

The still silent
trajectory over
earth's languid
wail.

Blossoming
into
ocean-hued night …

Over the shadows
of moons,
which are
still
too delicate
in the
night wind.

Like
a baby's cry,
hovering
on the
threshold of angels.

Jupiter

Grass doesn't grow here
under nightlights,
rust hovered through the haze,
still wondering
how long I have been
humming
that simple old tune you
sang once
back when your
hands were smooth
as water,
and stroked a mandolin
like a waiting child,
waiting to be clothed;
rivulets of you...

Wavering up
and out
through the
old screen door,
under the light
of seven moons.

Mercury

Purple notes
of laughter
caught on my chin,
dripping like flowers
into the grass
through the stained glass
of your heart-worshipful
sky:
arctic-clear.

Venus

Wildflowers
stuck
to your hooped skirt
as you waded by...

Through the wild grass
hoping to find
a nice
mossy spot,
just quiet enough
(without thunder)
for a picnic
under the apple-green leaves
and dappled sunlight.

Mars

Footprints across
the red brick garden path
lend themselves to the
hum-hum
of scarlet
tulip-cupped bees.

Dahlias whispering
to each other
over the slow notes
of spring,
brush golden.

HALO OF THE BLUE GARDEN

House of Plum Tree

On the old
pathway under the stars,
the trees glisten in the darkness,
and the wind hovers gently
like mist, and
all the words you say seem soft and
radiant
against the night;
breathing the cold,
and glittering like
shooting
violet
fire.

House of the Blue Spruce

Under the night,
cool and soft,
remembrances like
dreams slide
over the shadows, and into
the diamond-studded
darkness;
when I breathed
you seemed distant,
and when I held my
breath,
the moon shades of dun,
your eyes deepened,
and grew into
vast
pools like
bottomless
stone lilies.

House of the Waterlily

Saturn, after
the haze,
reels,
dipping and spooning
into blue-green
flights,
like ocean flowers
spinning under
the night.

House of the Black Locust

Marrying peace and
distress like
a canopied pair,
two branches
mend and tear,
and grow wider
under struggle—
losing their leaves,
together, as a spray
over the hard earth,
seeking cover.

House of the Magnolia

Knotted, your hair
swings back,
bobbing against
the crowd,
under the Ferris wheel of
lights and parade.

Your eyes as ripe
as wisteria,
flowering bloom
in all directions,
you escape
convention,
and flourish.

House of the Dogwood

The ornamental duck,
sitting
under the rain, washed
like raiment cool and
wheat-brown,
dipped and floated,
and haunted the
majestic waters
with old dreams
and broken,
vanilla
feathers.

House of the Arbutus

Spinning
down papery
wishes,
like soft spools
of orange and sage.

From the bow,
I see an age-rounded
glossy sun,
with orange-blue
brass,
ringing notes,
like peals
of glassy
thunder.

House of the Willow

Starry and smooth,
lingering echoes
of beauty and
solace,
your curves
shift the
moonlight
to other shades of
tranquility:
china pools
spun with
threads from
d'Antans.

House of the Rhododendron

Rising under
twilight,
long and straight,
your hair—
hand-loomed,
little doves,
your notes
sweep into the
silence.

The black piano
stood still
in the empty room,
while you were
threading the ribbons
in angel's hair.

Rachmaninoff,
waiting to be heard,
and led like
soft stray kittens,
tumbling about
the yard,
bright
at dusk.

House of the Oak

Under the
honeysuckle,
dripping knots of summer
fragrance,
the swing buckles
against my legs, and
the hum of grass, blowing onto
the sidewalk, curtains
the silver sounds
of nocturne—
silent, so sweet,
and last whisper
vanishing.

House of the Silver Birch

One green riverbank
led to another world,
silenced by the thorns;
my dress torn,
the birdseed,
recklessly,
recklessly,
scattered ...
while magpies
fluttered
about the cool
stone bench.

Nothing to say,
the diligent,
thwarted;
soon the edges
were lisps
on my small
tongue, and my
harp, a chorus of gold lines,
fumbling in the dark
under sunrise-sunset:
the mist
of the presence
eluding our senses
like ice.

HALO OF THE DOOR

The Fragrance of Glory

A silhouette of man embroidered
his thoughts against the night:
we were waiting for heaven
in the dim blue,
and thought it good to wait,
possible to hope;
trees with their soft lips
touching the water, aqua,
again and again,
and fish swaying lazily
onward
in a fragrant world—
encompassed and vivid.
Bright like stars,
our eyes deepened,
noble and humble,
relinquishing heart
unto humanity's
gray tides
with such simplicity.

The Cottage

Soft and breathed,
silver-spun like
flaxen gold, this petal
wraps its stillness
like opals
from our eyes,
our thoughts opaque;
we thought the
baby,
dimming
beeswax, had
burned low.

Blinded, we ate poorly
in waiting and listened:
the birds cooed softly,
the night wept still,
and wrapped around my
little finger was
his hand.

Waterhouse

Miranda stood upon the sand once,
and the sapphire waves watered
her shore—tear-bright sea,
listless and drawn,
her mahogany mane
a blue canvas...
now the shipwrecked soul
is akin to the heart
with no veil.

O My Sweet Rose,
in the garden of
a thousand vales,
bathing in fine bergamot.

Golden Ophelia
upon the waterlily,
a deathly bed—
hollow and pale,
I tortured you;
the Lady of Shalott,
floating down the river
under a tapestry.

Destiny,
in pen and paint,
in candle's light,
I carved you, statuesque
in the radiance of time.

Chorus

The rivulets of
streams, carrying underground
treasures, twinkled
in laughs under and over
bridges made of matchsticks.
Dressing the morning
world with silver,
they, unified, rang:
in color,
my house beneath,
filled with
the translucence
of morning's glory.

Lithograph

Once you
looked at me
in sepia from
beneath the oak,
like a man stenciled against
the sky
and whispered
a silence;
on the waterway,
footsteps of
blue and azure
tile the
staircase we climb
under
snow-fragile
stars
to heaven.

Sky Quilt

Star dreams dotted
a vivid meadow
and caressed your
head like a baby's,
nestled in a cloud,
enveloping
a patchwork kite.

I sat and made daisy chains
in the grass,
decorating the neck
of a goddess
filled with platitudes
and beatitudes,
with long hippie hair
and a bandana,
making dandelion tea.

Firebird

The dawn creased
and flew away
over the sea
like a night bird
flying
back to where the skies
bend with stars:
I watched it go
and sadly
could not miss it
as the diamonds from its
beak fell on my soft head
and left dents
and crevices
like moonbeams.

Visitor

One night
the fire kindled,
a frost blew at the door;
it opened,
and there he was—
draped from head to foot
with a glowing mantle:
back from the sky
in hues of fire
with soft delight.

Quill

Still, so
still and white
like seashells, washed
by the salt
under the weave
of ocean sounds
echoing
and sanding
the designs of man
off eternity.

Once in a dark womb,
now you write:
and the notes are
eternal black;
toe shoes,
a pirouette
on an old
pine floor.

Evening

Under the stone arches
just where the pathway
ends
and light begins,
the aurora borealis
bench
in a courtyard
of color,
foxgloves and hollyhocks
still enamored in the
evening,
one sonatina
per child:
in our enclosure,
brick by brick—
winter garden,
autumn garden,
summer garden,
spring.

Liturgy

Browned and waiting
for olive
wine that would drip and
pour, we sang
1,700 years:
and the trees echoed lightly
as wind stirs;
wounded reeds bent
at the vision,
and eloquence breathed
deeply like a burning
star,
heralded to night
in royal
velvet.

HALO OF THE DAFFODIL

Eucalyptus

———

Teal
blue
clouds:
I sat
on the
scaffolding once
and painted
the sky.

White Angelica

An aluminum
boat,
rising
and falling
to the waves of
sea mist:
green and
gray,
capturing
rain.

Fennel

Little bird,
flying out
from
under the tangle of vines,
into the wide
open
world.

Juniper

Annexed to
the next
big
cedar,
like a
cross,
we pan
gold
amid the
rush
of clear water
and sunset.

Geranium

Where I
wander,
the light
falls
so softly,
as angels
in the twilight;
each china doll
a memory
of Noel.

Vetiver

Dust of
the ashes
of incense and
smoke lingering in the
room of black and
white portraits
simple, crisp
and the flutter
of eyelashes:
ripples
weighted on a shore.

Rosewood

Purple,
pink
hues the gorge
flowers
in rain-patterned
song;
picnics
under
the
blossoming.

Tansy

Sky
so bright,
like rust
and violet,
brimming
to the
horizon,
fair and bright.

Orange

Round and swift
like a fresh-squeezed sun,
tethering the wind
sweeping the valley
dotting the grove with cool
fragrance,
fading at nightfall,
drops of pewter oil.

Petitgrain

Washing
the
yellow
sun
over the bloom
of wisteria,
you
sparkle silver
like a thousand
volumes
never written.

German Chamomile

Cream and
silver court the night:
a flock of noble sheep,
tended
through the
galaxy
by the shepherdess.

Laurus Nobilis

Baby
eyes
spoken
into
understanding,
your verse
is a lullaby
in the night,
reaching heaven's
door.

Pepper

Wrinkle lights
your wind
to fire,
and like
a candle,
you burn
sepia.

Mountain Savory

Emerald
voices
jar
the
soft-spoken
evening
from afar,
whirling
the
deep
into rubbings
of cinder.

Lemonbalm

Peacock,
you bronze
hope after dream
into radiant
eye feathers,
to sweep
humanity
with the
brushstrokes
of
light.

Melissa

A fire
was built
from matches,
the soft
papery
lights around
you,
echoing with
solace.

Lavender

Patterns,
painted
blue and white,
paper the wall
with
fragrance
and Victoriana.

Ginger

Hearth
stills the daze
under
honey skies,
to plaid blankets
and
wood-warm
flickers.

White Balsam

Blinded,
searching for
a flower
under the
snow,
I
miss
white flowers
falling
out of
the
sky.

Tsuga

Icicles
fringe
the rooftops:
craggy eyebrows
over the
eve
lights.

Clary Sage

Fragrant mist
steeps
the garden
into
rich ripened
tapestries,
like the
sea
on a
midsummer's
night.

Rose

A canopy
of lightness,
pearl
blossoms
unfurl
to antiquity,
the violinist
poised
on an old
stone
wall.

Patchouli

Rambling
through the measure
of wood and stream;
my boyhood
journeys
cost me
no more than
a piece of string,
a pocket knife,
and an old
water spout
from the pump
by
the
well.

Peppermint

Trailing the
watering can
over the wall,
and on into summer's pathway—
gardens
sang, as I
watered the
medieval
herbs.

Helichrysum

The northern pines
dappled
.the
moonlight,
and caribou
herded
through
rivers
of castile
waters and
echoes of
tundra,
over the
salmon
returning
to spawn.

Cloves

Skies
lit my
hazel eyes to
bronze,
under
the oak
where you
waited
like
dream
rainbows, melting
in a glassblower's
shop.

Cinnamon Bark

Stillness
split the
stone of my
soul,
hazing
the crispness
of clear color
into
cindery
hearts.

Bergamot

The
wrinkled depths
of
your burnished
smile
erase
the smears
of
yesterday,
etching my gray into
portraits of
Scottish
grace.

Ylang Ylang

Entering
the places of space,
takes courage
beyond
hope,
and streaks in a weary sky
where Ophelia
glided
placidly
by.

Ravensara

The things
we
do
test us
to free
our dreams,
and places,
nested deep—
to hold
the stained glass,
the Latin,
the golden moon.

Valor

Under the
knight cloak,
ruddy
and decorated
with valor,
you turn into
my radiant hero:
war-wearied,
and
true
enough to kiss.

Ledum

A poem floating downstream
is seldom found,
but
swallowed by a large fish,
it swims on past and to the
seas of poems,
swimming on past.

Goldenrod

Daffodils
sweep the gold
over the
emerald fields of
mountain
glory,
rich as kings.

HALO OF THE MORNING

Prelude

Under me,
you swim the tides
of oceans,
climb
jagged
rock like a mountain
goat and whisper
of trees in the
wind.
Under my heart,
I breathe into your
silence,
breaking the
dusk with
poignancy
and dedicated
song.

Lullaby

Where I lay
my head
the straw is
warm and dry,
but scratches
where I am most soft,
like warm
dewy-down heather.

And the earth under
the mist
reels
with acceptance
and rejection,
starlight bathes
my forehead,
as a tattered crown,
and leaves twist
aimlessly
to my
bosom:
reaching
to earth
from

heaven
like
pearls
falling
in the
night.

Minuet

Under the
reaches of
humanity,
a little girl
sang simple
songs and waited
for birth.
She nursed him
like the wildflowers
in her cloak,
and wished
to know why
angels ruffled
their brightness
in such
humble
cottages.
By the fire,
her lenten
pottage
grew.

Study

What fine hair
covers me
and softens my
wails to
whispers:
her eyes to mine,
glowing
solace
in the frost
like
the ebony
stencil of
trees against
a bare sky.

Étude

Mastering your
chin, the
dimples
stutter softly
across the chaos
and silence the night;
stars push into being
over the rhapsody
of the eternal;
rivuletted to
pour into
my gentle
homely
chest.

Concerto

Naked, screaming
your furor,
you dance under
the sky
like a wildman
lotus.

In dreams,
staring across the
open field,
I see the many
eyes that
bathe you,
the webbed tides,
always to hold
you back,
and the
cushions of
sage grass,
to heal you
again and again
from your
own fury.

Requiem

The velvet-strung
night,
rippling with the
weight of such
madness,
a drunk king
jealous with
fright and his
own gold.
Bristling as a hair
on a camel's back, I
wander through
the
corridors of stars
losing hope after
hope like
stray moons
withering on a
glassy plain.

Symphony

One glory
fell
as a
stone—
impenetrable
and caked
with earth
into my
bosom
as it
rooted to
life
deeper
than my life
and tears,
diamond rimmed.

Gregorian Chant

This one,
white and pure
with eyes
that see;
soft and cloaked
with godhood…

Little,
unknowing
the rivers
that stream
to your
heart
from mine.

Toccata

Unpreceded
you rise,
blue in darkness,
lighting a way
not lit by
mortality,
and the
almond flower
of your
fragile bloom grows
deeper
with each
teardrop.

Song

Simple and poor,
like earth
tousled
under the sun,
wood-burnished
and spare—
your hands would stretch
and piece together
joy.

Mazurka

I kneel and
the fire
burns softly,
like a cloak
under which
I rest,
dusty,
smoky;
my hands,
weathered,
tired, and
crook
harnessing
my soul
to God.

Song Without Words

Stars lit
your royalty
long before
I saw you kneel,
and let go
the outward streams
of glory
for the deeper
inward song.
Along your journey
you flew,
to the waiting
childlike womb—
reaching skyward
for a kiss
from
light.

Orpheum

Quickened
I bow,
royal-hued
and tapered,
wreathed with gold,
to graze the sights,
the constellations
of a newer-born
sky.
His eyes betray
the scarlet eggs,
my emerald robe,
drifting
earthwards
and in my hands,
perfumed,
the fan
of a peacock's tail
imbues
the dark ebony
of my weary,
drawn
face;
shimmering in the
depths of the
azalea pools,
a garden,
in the moonlight:
shadowed in the
glimmer—
I bade him
flight.

Fugue

Under the moon
the kind sand cools
to liquid dust;
like snakes,
the tall reeds sway and catch
at my sandals.

The blisters pain my brow
drops of crimson,
and your soft
eyes echo
the grueling
heartache
of your childlike mother's
tears:
pewter rain
into the
silence
of the shadow.

Aria

The sun's might
sets the world
on edge,
a tiger,
waiting to pounce
and tear
and devour:
the sand dust
breathes in my eyes,
quenching
my thirst to
fire.
In the night, strewn with
stars like eyes,
we watch the
distant galaxies,
dreaming of
faraway cities
like ice.

Opera

Myrrh is a kiss
straight from God,
resting on your chest
in the deep.

You were chosen
from the beginning,
and now all of time
rests in you.

The chronology
of destiny
unveils its ministering
arm of light
upon this stage.

Morning to night,
the adoration of nature—
ocean to mountain—
is unceasing in its praise.

Cantata

Boy-child
your smile
is water, poured
into my
thirsty heart
as if a
cactus
had split the
sky in
worship
of you.

Minor

One stone
I sit upon
in this
vast
oasis—
fronds
swaying
like shadows over
the sky,
blue as
amethyst—
hard and cold
and white;
waiting
for
a gardener.

Harmony

In the beginning,
I loved you
and carried
you in my
arms,
like a sleeping child
out of
Egypt.
Wanting to wake you
to my solace,
I bequeathed
to you
vision upon
vision out of the
night,
like stars,
pulsed into being
under the
laughter
of the eternal light
of a young king
looking for
joy
and
amazement.

Hymn

In the evening,
stars
still lingering
over the
olive tree,
your head
shines
under the
canopy of night;
and like a
copper stallion,
your oil
flows,
coursing
through
the dust
and
ancient
cobblestones,
to wipe
the streets
with silver.

Interlude

In the
presence
of kings
light falls over
thee,
diamonds
from an ancient
sky
braided thee,
desert,
crimson,
gold,
ripples from
the streams
betrothed thee,
into the sand
of light
and shadowing;
echoing
voices
in the thundering,
spilling
over the cool sands
into my
own
captivity and
light.

HALO OF THE ICON

Hyssop

Ribbons
in the rain
of soft pearls
like
echoes across
the canyons
of deep.

Sea after sea,
to breathe
and take rhythm
like old
shepherds,
crook in arm,
wandering on a
song-drenched hillside.

Onychra

Joseph
couldn't have
asked for better:
one beautiful
life
echoing my
song,
and raiment
like snow.

Under the tree
I watch you
move with the
wind
like the wine of olives
and your intricate
heart breathes,
a moon in a
silken sky.

Cassia

Berries in the
dust
charm their
way into the
multitude's hands;
palms sweating
with diseases lick
my fingers
while
ravens
soar in
arcs
over the
nuanced
oasis.

Aloes

Like you
I am healed
under the joy
of love
and washed
by this same
fountain;
a thousand years
and I could sit here
still
on this same
old hill ...

The cypress trees glistening
in the darkness
as the earth
shines
under the
unwieldy
sky of morning
waiting
to rise.

Myrrh (The Apostle John Observes)

In the breadth of
sky
that ripens
like an
olive branch...

Whispers over
the wall of sorrow
falling like the
dreams of
yesterday—

Every breath you breathe
seems poised against
a sky of tears,
and voices
cry
out from the
earth,
of injustice nailed
to an olden
weighted song.

Branch for branch,
it reaches across the
gathering dusk,
and piercing through
the whitened ripples,
all is strung ...

Horror across the
tight-lipped
fragile face
of God, too naked
for all man
to scoff.

Galbanum

Aching, the
cold stone kneels
in my heart,
emptying
my feverish
prayer
to silent
whispers.

By night they came
and bound me
to my own
stricken
vow.

Like an animal,
I bowed under
their darkness,
and steeled
I cracked and
shook
with blood ...

Violence streaming
down my
chin,
all my rights
crucified,
like the bitter snares,
I looked on
them
and blessed them,
wild with
fury.

Spikenard (Mary Magdalene)

Blossoming the
night pale,
I wander through
the galaxies of silver,
still;
orchids
crystallize in
milky
progression
overhead,
and the memories
of you
dip and spoon,
fragrant oil
down
my ebony hair.

Where you hung,
the earth seems
tried and subdued,
mountains, solemn,
wreathed with dust,
the rockrose wilts.
And olives fall like
meteors into the
silence;
under the shadow,
stillness falls
like rain.

Myrtle

This night has no darkness,
only infinite frailty,
under
the realms of no
return.

In the stillness of death,
I release my breath
into the
heartache;
aching,
pierced,
I wander
draped with loss.

Cistus

Twinkling lights,
angels under heaven
take flight
in the
shell-shallow
pools
of tide water.

Salty like breath,
they cling to
my shadows,
and children as
ghosts
pass before
my being.

On the cross,
I carried them back
to the throne,
like old sleeping willows—
out of the night
to solace.

Weeping, they
came
back from the depths,
to kiss
the nest of plenty,
in all the grace
of long-suffering
and fleur-de-cœur...

Whispering their solemn
perfume,
how they asked of me,
my hands,
and feet,
to press their scars
to mine.

Mint flowers in their hair,
they joined
the dance
of time and
mystery,
where wrong calls nothing
its own,
and the mist of
heaven
pierces our eyes
and soul
beyond the grave.

Frankincense

You wake me
with the dawn
like glorious
hope into the
streams
of glory.

A cave of wonder,
my sodden grave, now
flaxen, but
a chrysalis.

Rose of Sharon

Pounding my
hopes into
a new grave
I rejoiced
at the life
always
on each
side of sacrifice—

For the Father
calls his own
out of the
night
of no
return.

Vision shook my being
like a shooting star,
and in His hand
I strung the
galaxies.

Like each star,
named, we enter
into the royal
halls;
steeped under the
love of a thousand ages
we rise,
back from the dead
in the harmony of each
of the holy oils
of galbanum, onychra, aloe,
myrrh, frankincense, cassia
cistus, spikenard, myrtle.

HALO OF OTHERWORLDS

I.

———

In this silence,
the stars burn still,
and shadows seep
under the woods to
clothe me with the
joy of worlds;
and when the presence looms
out of the field of ravishing,
your hair
blows in a wind of currents
beyond dreams,
and all my truth resounds
into heaven.

The dust of earth
cakes a man to the ground:
his substance,
poised on the brink
of otherworlds,
and under his heart,
simple as a plow, lie
two children,
hand in hand.

II.

See
how the trees whip and bend their
multicolored leaves into
dishes of song:
roses blossom
in the park,
petals all in a line,
then
winter breathes
too soft,
honey white
under the branches
draped with snow, and kept
a cool green
eucalyptus,
the stillness—
radiant and
hopeful,
like a bride.

III.

The jewels
crease the night,
like glass beads
of a rosary,
under the ecumenical crown
of the archaic church.

Twinkle twinkle
little star—
in graffiti
over the train station;
two Jews on a platform,
with heavy brown shoes,
dark hair,
and knitted conifer
satchels.

This one night
each star
rippled and too crisp
prismed
into sure
clear nothingness.

IV.

Watering my garden,
each shoot,
a child,
waiting for rain.

Colorful and fragrant
into the dawn,
they stretch their hands.

Ponds,
in a circular motion,
tissue paper,
to cover my
black eyes,
ovens deep.

Oils of Olay,
angels in sepia,
framed in wood,
from an old
book of knowledge—
black, and gold
gilt edges.

V.

White and tiny
millefleurs
in a poor woman's basket:
eggs like opals,
rounded and fair.

Like hard green nuts,
the fruit fell
to the ground.

The spindles of a
tansy garden,
stonewalled.

VI.

Blue and
gauzy
under the vines
of pale sweet peas,
something borrowed
without words,
forget-me-nots,
in one handkerchief.

A queen's boudoir:
light perfume,
through the
open casement
window.

VII.

Dried red
on display in an old
backstreet gallery,
hurtling through
five stops and
two trams,
the blue blotches
ran.

One framed portfolio per Jew;
one star,
our Galileo,
a million dollar man,
chaste of virtue—leaning
on an old leather case,
fleets, white-haired
and counted.

VIII.

Trains rumbling
into the dark,
the eastern journey
grew dim in my
eyes, but
somewhere in the
deep as hell
agnostic cavity, one alone
crosses our silence.

Our song rose into
the night;
it was a pure
and powerful song:
it spoke of a hope
that could not be forgotten:
the hope of youth,
the hope of innocence—
one thousand strong,
in the shadow
of the Fatherland.

IX.

This day,
the sun sets to carry us
across a passage, into
another dream and story,
like a wind
in a vale of poplars.

The boats landed, and
I swim, together with you,
and you hold my back,
breaching me like a
whale, too deep,
rising to surface.

X.

Under this sun, so bright,
and the stars indivisible,
and the night, fathoms away
across the channels of oceans,
too vast to cross—
you stand
back to back, like soldiers
in the sands,
waiting for nothing
but breathing.

XI.

Star-flower: you bend
a million nights
steady.

HALO OF THE RUNE

Out of the Wind

Out of the wind
of mountains,
the tears
trailing
from the streams of sky;
antelope gather,
far-reaching,
reaching,
wandering gold—
azure and silver,
on the north hill,
how the lights reel—
far-reaching,
reaching,
the antelope,
gathering,
gathering,
under the storm.

Africa

I relished white
desert mouth,
open like
a lion, roaring,
early in
February once;
the moon,
a silver dime,
the wind,
a wild horse,
and the fields,
overgrown with cotton,
sang spirituals in their
chains.

The wallpaper
was flecked with print
(pattern and texture)
like horses,
whispering,
(white on white)
whispering,
into the night.

Tiny Shell Runes

Mostly from nature:
mother-of-pearl,
stem-glass buttons,
a bird's bed, coral in color—
the lauder sun,
lighting the reading chair.

Fire screen,
made from canvas
stretchers, stitched together,
deft quilted cotton,
the blue grosgrain,
ribboned—
tapered green walls,
a quirky waltz;
the transfiguration
of white down the staircase,
flowers, in odyssey,
sea biscuits
on the tea table,
warming the essential.

Eloquent, and just
cream
on pewter enamel:
a very English
garden, hedged;
boxed pansies—
in daiquiri
ice and chocolate.

Mist over Heaven

A stone-sacred
hearth,
mulling
the crackling pine,
welcoming the tapestry
of feathered cedar;
the still,
the silent,
vibrant wind,
brown and white
crockery,
unruffled
on the table—
my baskets
of ivy,
trailing
under my arm,
as I elope
unto the heather,
unto the gray
cliffs,
osprey
circling
into
the mist.

On Golden Pond

Under my list
of memories,
resides a mounted
iris,
the scuffed floorboards
dressed with leather
shoes,
an oasis
under the dark-wood
stairs.

The gathered sun,
a stone hearth;
my skin as fine as
parchment paper,
straightens,
then blurs,
as I turn my face
quickly toward
the morning.

Slow Enough to Dance

The hills,
moon-brushed with sorrow—
spires, knee-high,
captured the traces
of rocky mountain,
spun with sage;
into the morning,
the meadow larks
rose and flung
their nuances.

Rosen gold,
the windows
drape your solace,
the tears
taper your bricks,
one by one
into the darkness.

The Young Ophelia

Down under the rushes
blue,
the streams of rushes
to carry you,
idyll of my soul,
so prism and true,
still and pale,
in green like sky.

And where the road was
wreathed with dust,
the peasants traveled
from far off, their
horns ablaze,
their call to arms.

I but a lad,
had no new clothes,
but in my hand
I held the world.

HALO OF THE FUGUE

Paper Blossom: fugue

I.

On the table,
you may be a
crock of butter.

In the living room,
an arranged
vase of flowers.

But all things bright
and beautiful…

You were born
out of sight,
out of mind,
and into
the dawn of time.

II.

Under the mesh of
wails,
we pray
things like
songs,
riveting the
darkness.

Under the birds,
intricate, cooing
their continents
in verve,
we still
the chaos
of the night.

III.

Like moons
from the sky,
like violet,
when my world
encompassed this one,
through the pain, interminable,
I would meet death.

And scarce sanctities
in marble halls, silhouette...
ribboned to a
bird without wings,
under eves,
rising.

That the rippled hush
of spring—
falling rain, out of the trees
of snow, would find
a rose, to crush,
and pierce,
and failing,
desert...

From stone,
into the
face of
light.

REFERENCE NOTES

THE LAUREL WREATH

The Door

Lund, Chris. Textual excerpts from the publication: *A photographic essay on Canada's Houses of Parliament: Stones of History*. Ottawa: National Film Board of Canada, 1967. Reproduced with permission from the National Film Board of Canada.

CONTACT

The Emily Isaacson Institute
P.O. Box 3366
Mission, B.C. Canada
V2V 4J5

www.emilyisaacsoninstitute.com